# IN THE FINANCIAL DISTRICT

# IN THE FINANCIAL DISTRICT

POEMS BY
*Ralph Pomeroy*

The Macmillan Company / New York
Collier-Macmillan Limited / London

Library of Congress Catalog Card Number: 68-19825

First Printing

The Macmillan Company, New York
Collier-Macmillan Canada Ltd., Toronto, Ontario
Printed in the United States of America

*The author wishes to express his gratitude to the MacDowell Colony and to Mr. George Kendall, its administrator, for a fellowship granted to him.*

### ACKNOWLEDGMENTS

Many of the poems in this volume were first published in the following magazines, anthologies, and books: *Arts in Society, Botteghe Oscure, New American Review, Prairie Schooner, The Listener, The London Magazine, The Northwest Review, The Observor, The Paris Review, Southern Poetry Review, The Times Literary Supplement, Transatlantic Review.*

The poems "October," "2 P.M. Going Westward on the Chicago, Burlington & Quincy" and "High Wind at the Battery" appeared originally in *The New Yorker.*

The following poems first appeared in *Poetry*: "Confession," "For Your Vase" (part a. as part 6 and part e. as a section of part 5 in "Diary of a Moveable"; part i. as a section of "Lakes Learn from the Season"), "Kite Flying," "Letter to Pasternak," "Looking at the Night" (a shorter version of "Out of the Window Into Moonlight"), "Overwhelmed by the Moon at the Wrong but Imperative Moment," "Sentry Seurat," "The King of the Wild Beasts," "The Novelist at Home in New Jersey," "To My Father" (as part 4 of "Diary of a Moveable") and "To Words." "Columbus" is reprinted with permission from *FOCUS/Midwest*, copyright 1963, FOCUS/Midwest Publishing Company, Inc. The poem "The Tuilleries" first appeared in *The New Statesman.*

The following poems first appeared in anthologies: "Corner" and "In the Redwood Forest" in *A Controversy of Poets* (Anchor Books, 1965), copyright 1961 by Ralph Pomeroy; "Trying to Sleep" in *Eight Lines and Under* (The Macmillan Company, 1967), copyright 1965 by Ralph Pomeroy. Other poems first appeared in *Stills & Movies* (Gesture Press, 1961), copyright 1961 by Ralph Pomeroy, and *The Canaries As They Are* (Charioteer Press, 1965), copyright 1965 by Ralph Pomeroy.

*To my dear family, dead and alive*
*To my dear friends, near and far*

# CONTENTS

## *IN THE FINANCIAL DISTRICT*

## *TOWARD*

# FIRST TIMES

# FIRST TIMES

I AM trying to get
to the bone of the body
which I've never been able
to get at because of walls.

The body itself is a wall
(and things wall-in the body)
not to mention the mind.

And where is the heart
in all this?
And where is the soul?
What eyes do I need?
What skills to probe?

And why do I need to get there?
And what will be waiting?

If I think there is bone there
I must *know* something.
Where did I get the idea?
O where did I catch the inkling?

I am haunted by deathless primaries,
by thoughts of some super-clear,
by dim experiences of first times . . .

O childhood, my primeval!

# COLUMBUS

He sets forth often in my mind.
Particularly in October when
my birthday falls, together with the leaves,
on the day named after him.
Maybe some whim of research chose the twelfth
from the stack of Open Dates
left on the official desk.

I enjoy picturing him—
and those ridiculous ships
dipping along in prophetic Indian file
like an animated cartoon.

With absolute faith
(shaken most when the fresh fruit
ran out) he lied about the number
of days gone by. To himself his math
was a grey anxiety darkening into fear.
Yet he willed the world round.
He was certain of that
curved line becoming a plane:
he saw the waters unroll into flatness
all around him—
to that line!

*Water! Skies!*
*My hand on the wheel,*
*my eyes*
*for the back door of the Indies. . . .*

His ships fell westward
like three sunsets, but stayed

afloat. One of his men swayed
out from the crow's-nest in the moonlight.
The Captain General prayed—
to the holy traveler whose name he was given—
remembered his own last name,
looked to heaven,
and thought "doves". . . .

About the mast
a white blurring.

Gulls!

During the sixth glass of the watch
a voice cried from the rigging. . . .

Land arrived.

# TO MY FATHER

May the Milky Way enter my Father's fading eyes
in which, as a child, I journeyed across seas as white
and blue as those at the Great Poles.
May sunlight find its house in his smile.
May clocks dance in his heart.
May roses bloom in his wine.
May hollyhocks climb his chair.
May the telephone sing him songs.
May lettuce amuse his lips.
May gardens send him engraved invitations to their
openings.
May darkness when it unfolds
presage only a field for stars.

# KITE FLYING

THE kite at the end of the string in his hand
holds the other end of a rope
that turns as the wind jumps over it in a game
played in the bright yard that lies between cloud and head.

Earlier he sent a message up its thin slope
carefully written and folded. It went, "I love you."
Now he pretends he's forgotten who it is to,
but wonders if he'll get an answer from anyone.

Over an orchard of downed Northern Spies,
rotting in boozy heaps by the old quarry,
the lax string carries his letter, his worry.
It travels like a country train, forever stopping.

Anyhow, suddenly, he starts to wind in,
watching and jerking the string skillfully,
carefully hauling the green tissue diamond down—
always away from the trees, playing the line.

Then he sits down and winds like a spinner
busy with golden threads and no nonsense.
And as his message slowly comes back to him,
the wind sends it away and he goes home reasonably to
            dinner.

# LIZARDS (?)

THERE were two of them
one morning after rain
on the way to the hill barns.

The first one, there, at my feet,
as I walked the drying stones,
the first, surprised me—

being small, perfect and bright red
exactly like the little frogs
and lizards my nephew turns out

with his plastic molding set.
Even a lot like gum candy
with its lovely semi-transparent color.

I thought some child had dropped it,
bored, from the back seat of a car
where he was playing.

But then, halfway up the steep
drive that leads to the barns
I saw the second—the same size!

About three inches long with four
short legs, feet spread like hands,
and marked with faint black dots.

Looking close, I saw its
dark, heavy-lidded eyes,
half-closed like a sleepy child's.

Two was too strange. So, a bit fearfully
(why?), I blew gently on it
and it moved! Just the merest motion.

Others told me that I had seen
chameleons. (Of course!)
I looked forward to them

when I walked back down from the barns.
But the road-builders had passed
and there was no sign of them.

# WINDOW POEM

A BEE is climbing
the Venetian blind
like a ladder.

He knows the air
the sun, the garden
are out there.

But
this cool, clear wall
somehow
prevents him
from getting to
the bees that knock
against the other side
like tossed pebbles.

Then I, God,
go over
and open the window.
And he finds the chink
in the crystal barrier
and zooms out.

A gust of flies
taps at the invisible wall
along with the bees
who keep at it.

A white flower,
one of a bunch in the garden,

flutters, trembles
and joins the dance
on the pane,

slipping down suddenly
now and then
like a small-time
shooting star.

# A FROG, LEAPING

LEAPING, you leave a fit of crystal
rallying, in eddies, for the next disturbance.
      Startled lilies regain their delicate balance,
preening for their blue images, shaking dry.

      The sky simply lifts you and lands you.
You are not so much yourself as an emblem
      of dainty riskers, floating high on wires.
In a different circus you'd jump in spotlights.

      But you're lucky. When you drop,
you don't fall into a bowl of hoarse voices,
      but dive into weaving crowds of green.
O emerald acrobat! Your hazard is not down but up.

# LIFE OF AN APPLE

An apple drops, out of control.
Maybe it will be found and shined—
or left where it lies
surrounding an occupant worm
which fattens on its adopted parent like a long child.

Around it, like disciples or star systems,
blown seeds continue their cycles.

Motionless it waits, rots
and sweetens in the ground.

# SOLDIER'S REST

When he got back from The Service
he had no limp,
he had no scars
to show.

Nights, he rocked on a Northern Lake
cradled in the neat pod of a canoe . . .

And watched the small stars at their wars—
unreachable, for now.

# BETWEEN HERE AND ILLINOIS

WHEN my father died
I didn't get my brother's telegram.

Tuesday, the day my sister called,
I wasn't home.
It was sunny at the beach.

On Wednesday I got up at eight,
drank a glass of cold Tropicana,
had raisin toast, instant coffee,
went off to work.

That day my brother flew my father's body
from San Fernando to Illinois.

The rest of the week went by.
I was home all the following Sunday
because it was too cold to go swimming.

Monday, my sister reached me.
In the atmosphere of my office
I heard her voice, all the way from Michigan.

She said that the funeral was over.
She described the black vestments and white flowers.
She said that they had all missed me
and were wondering where I was.

If they had reached me
I could have flown from New York to Illinois—

all the way from here to Illinois—
over all the graves that lie between here and Illinois.

# LOVE AND OTHER DISAPPOINTMENTS

# US

*to J-P*

LOVERS, certain
we were making a new shape
cut and fabricated out of hours
whose size had no limit
but just continued outward at both sides,
we set-up for always.

Happiness!

Joy, like released dye,
spread as in water.
We swam, we sailed
outward on it—expanding
like the stars.

Time was gentled.
Even the formulas turned new.
Our days, our nights moved
through us like filters—purified.
Pure wakings. Pure gazes.

The formulas are tarnishing.
Time is galloping violently,
unbroken.
Even by us.

# CONFESSION

Love, I am guilty of listening to hotrods
practicing somewhere below the window
with you beside me, quiet as linen,
folded—lax with fondness.

And while you lie there
my mind is up and dressing
to follow my imagined body
already bounding,
like an echo,
down the stairs.

# PLEA

DON'T turn your head
or act like you're sorry
I'm here against your body,
baffled, interested.

Look instead
at my eyes looking . . .

Wonder what time the clock
is telling itself to point a hand to
over there in the dark
just past your pillow?

Jesus! your left leg felt
cold just now!
Do you want to run
away from all our heat?

Your arms and back are bare.
I mean, your half
of the blanket's half on the floor.

I hear a car.
Does it make any difference
to your silence?

What will make you happy?
O my dearest,
be free, be free!
Turn to me without fear!
Come to me as you are!

# WET JULY

DARK rain qualifying heat.
Summer aching to jump out.
Muffled.     Nipped.
We complain to each other.

When morning proves gray again
we cannot forgive it;
can't believe in any promising
swimming tadpoles of light we're given.
We long to bake and roast like loaves
while bees murmur—transistors in the trees.

Killer clouds reach down and quench.
Downpour again!

We stay pale.

# THE LAST FERRY OF THE SUMMER

WE move. And holiday goes off.
The blue belongings of summer are aboard and stowed.
Behind, suspended until our return,
the broken and locked lean.

Beyond the bulwark horizon, thunder retreats
to its flapping tents.
The sea and sky are one seamless opalescence.
The clouds of morning act out their calendar illustrations.

On the table of the bay, light is thrown
and spread with sloops and trawlers.
Searching its milky vistas, we lose
The low, receding island, our summer, and our apprehension.

And become light, pushing light before us
as though gloom couldn't touch us, didn't exist;
ignoring the blackness below the puncture
where a fish leaps, piercing toward brightness.

And we, enthralled, renounce last evening
with its encircling and fighting starlight,
as though darkness were a sacrament received
only by believers in nightfall.

# WHAT WILL BECOME OF US?

First the action of the sun lifting the water—
young and fluid—then giving it away as rain,
as its silver seeds, to lie and wait
for the cold to ripen it.     Sun and ice:
Soft.   Hard.   Soft . . .
Constant change without ever separating.

# LOVE SONG

Now the longest voyage begins.
The wind, bunched at your ankles,
pauses, freshens, sends you to me . . .

Displays of laughter sparkle the air.
The familiar listless nights are ended.

There are no colors on earth adept as yours—
marine to my blue, green to my emerald.

# OVERWHELMED BY THE MOON AT THE WRONG BUT IMPERATIVE MOMENT

If it's a question of making it happen
then I suppose ways can be found—

mechanics, skill, novelty
should be able to rouse the old lift and heave-ho.

But this is more complicated.
I thought, I hoped, you'd taken in

the color of the wedge of moon
orange over the West Side Highway.

Orange over all places as we walked
easily toward where it made its statement

bold against the blue dark.
Did you notice it? I didn't ask.

That's what I mean about complicated
I didn't ask.      I want to know.

It's that question that hangs here.
My having to ask it.      My not wanting to ask it.

# FIRE PIECE

WHAT burns burned
and what wouldn't, clung.

I heard the roof go.
Saw the iron bed redden,
the ice bucket boil.

Nothing seems able to fire my heart
though the skin of my bones roars.

# MIND'S GEOGRAPHY
*from the Polish of Adam Mickiewicz*

I AM a corpse sitting in your midst.
My eyes look into your eyes, I argue always,
but my soul, far off—oh far—strays,
a foreigner, star-fetching, fingering skies.

There is a country in me, mind's geography,
more beautiful than the one that meets my eye.
I have brothers and sisters, heart's family,
relationships dearer than any by blood.

I ditch my cares, my work, my fun,
wear shadows under willows out of the sun,
lie like an island on sweet grassy swells,
stalk sparrows and the sea shells' salt-bells—

Then sight her as she lights, white from the porch,
flickers through the meadow into the orchard,
floats in the wheat, weightless and water-clear,
shines, mountain-climbing, like the morning star.

# GONE

WIND rattles the apples.
The sky brims with sunset cider.
Field flowers, ash and maples,
dip like flags to the day's close.

No one gathers the wash.
No mice tattoo the cupboards.
There is no house with doors
springing to keep out flies.

Stones in the high weeds
mark where there was.

# GOODBYE

BITTER day. The sun's in. Wind
blasphemes against the windows.
Rain riots on the roof and weeps down all the mirrors.

I kneel and weigh the trunk lock into place,
rise and listen for the taxi.
And am alone, stranger to where I have lived
now that the rooms are empty of all that's left of me.

I hesitate and almost say something,
but a calling horn stops me;
sift slowly down the stairs like an ensemble of ashes;
pause, remembering sun in the windows,
and close the door as though opening others.

# LOCATIONS

# EXPECTING RAIN

WE move in a kind of container.
Even, unshaded light envelops us.
There is a persistent experience
of weightlessness everywhere.

Looking out through my glass wall of window
I feel everything is cupped—
my north stretch of woods included,
shadowless almost, except for the deepest entrances.

And all waiting for some god's hand
to suddenly turn it over
so that the repressed rain can fall.

# AUTUMNAL

*to Barbara and Elizabeth*

WE sit facing the October 3:30 sun
beside the half-empty pool—
half empty except for green brackish water,
dead leaves, willow reflections,
and the sun's dazzle.

A marbleized ball rests on a plastic chair.
The fly swatter lies inert.
A wasp circles the hot
seat of an empty chair.

Two sixtieth birthdays.
Two women, beautiful in their ways.

The cows meander about the gentle slopes.
The leaves do their colorful swan dives.

We sit facing the 3:30 sun.

# THIS HOTEL ROOM

THOUGH it is
in the thirties
outside,
it is hot
in here.
The window is
open wide
but
the heat
from the radiator
seems stronger.

Anyway,
my socks
are drying
toward
tomorrow
(which is
Sunday)
so I can't
turn the heat
off.

Daylight Saving
Time
ends
tonight.
And there has
been,
this week of
October,
snowfall.

Think of it!
This room,
without
a john or
shower,
but
with a bed
(single),
desk & chair,
dresser,
lamp,
sink,
closet,
window,
radio,
this cube
goes on
occupying space
as though it were
actually
becoming an hour
earlier
than it is,
as though
snow hadn't
fallen,
as though
I weren't
in it
at all.

# TRYING TO SLEEP

THERE is dark.
I can't hold it.
Dogs bark
down in the street.

I've shut the blind
but repeat
the cut of the moon
in my mind.

# BECALMED IN THE PICKWICK ARMS

WHAT's happening to me?
Every day I wake and click
the radio to news and
shave a stranger dying for coffee.

But the water in the faucet
isn't hot enough to make instant—
"No Cooking Allowed in This Hotel."

Rough weather in my mind.

Oblivious sleep is kind—
I dream and drift,
vacationing from what ails me.

Alarmed active,
I think I am alive
and struggle up because of it.

# CORNER

THE cop slumps alertly on his motorcycle,
supported by one leg like a leather stork.
His glance accuses me of loitering.
I can see his eyes moving like fish
in the green depths of his green goggles.

His ease is fake. I can tell.
My ease is fake. And he can tell.
The fingers armored by his gloves
splay and clench, itching to change something.

As if he were my enemy or my death,
I just stand there watching.

I spit out my gum which has gone stale.
I knock out a new cigarette—
which is my bravery.
It is all imperceptible:
the way I shift my weight,
the way he creaks in his saddle.

The traffic is specific though constant.
The sun surrounds me, divides the street between us.
His crash helmet is whiter in the shade.
It is like a bull ring as they say it is just before the fighting.
I cannot back down. I am there.

Everything holds me back.
I am in danger of disappearing into the sunny dust.
My levis bake and my T shirt sweats.

My cigarette makes my eyes burn.
But I don't dare drop it.

Who made him my enemy?
Prince of coolness. King of fear.
Why do I lean here waiting?
Why does he lounge there watching?

I am becoming sunlight.
My hair is on fire. My boots run like tar.
I am hung-up by the bright air.

Something breaks through all of a sudden,
and he blasts off, quick as a craver,
one with his power; watching me watch.

# FLYING FROM SAN FRANCISCO

Our backs turn
on the city.

After take-off,
only abstractions of water
racing below us.
The sun with us,
moving over the water—
running marigold
burning on the water.

Clouds above us,
in the water,
becoming chrysanthemums,
opening under water.

Beneath us now—
fields, roofs,
and diagonal great roads.
A river contradicting
the roads' attempt at
straight answers.

# LOCATION

Alone again. And here.
A foreigner alone again. Why here?

On invitation from a sweet stranger
you rode with the waves

from westward to eastward—
rode from a tangle to a clearing.

Or thought you did.
Or willed you would.

Riding you forgot why you were riding
and the motion took you and rocked you.

You were happy.
Maybe are happy now—though alone.

The movement turned you into a kind of song
or sound of singing made from water and wind.

And as a song you were most like yourself.
Or thought you were and were that nearer free.

You were the rocker and the rocking music.
The movement took you through its wavy changes.

And you became or un-became
and found your desire in those differences.

No thought of the shape of the target,
the color, smell, material of the target.

What shape has this place you occupy?
Isn't this land red and in an O?

# THE TUILLERIES

As the fountains falter and slip sideways,
bent downward by the weather to their basins,
children play. In a round pool,

toy boats (pushed outward) buckle and rush,
search for the other side, a welcoming harbor,
while I display my solitude over the back of a thin chair.
And the flowers grieve, fumble and shed color
downward in a fading rain.

While I sit watching the Louvre rust in the sun,
the boats (pushed outward) buckle and turn,
search for a corner, a goal for their larky voyage.
But curve after curve insists on a circular ocean.

While I slip sideways, bent downward by this weather,
fumble for songs, for an angular harbor-homing,
the world stays round.

# THE CONCERTS
*Forio d'Ischia, 1951*


EVERY afternoon a ritual of music
all by myself before the wireless
("radio" seems too modern a word for what it was),
descending light slanting to a point
where its beam balanced on my feet before
flattering the old tiles on its way down from the shutters.

And as the days went by the deaths
of afternoons became a mixture of fading light and music—
I seemed to be celebrating the passing days
as much as the concerts.

The women in the kitchen were getting the evening meal.
No one else was staying so early in the summer.
So I made a social hour and a change,
washing and shaving and putting on fresh clothes
in honor of the anticipated music broadcast
by the Italian Third Program,
in honor of the sunset.

Most of the women wore black and
seemed to be always busy.
I seemed idle to them, yet
I don't think they resented me.
After all, I was a young man and American
so I had to be rich: young men from America
were special and allowed to be unusual.
In a way they were unreal to those islanders—
arriving with too many trunks and going
for long solo walks in the company of lizards and poppies,
wandering through the high-noon, empty vineyards

up the mountain shaded by dust-and-silver olive trees
or along the breakwater, into the sailors' chapel
hung with votive boats—
keeping silent, eating alone,
arranging flowers everywhere in their rooms,
gazing at the sea as if to see all the way across it.

That's what I imagine them saying
to one another as they pummeled the laundry
or shoved wood into the stove.

I was like a traveler in a savage land
and I had to be very careful because I was afraid.
Therefore the little ceremonies to break the dangerous
                        repetitions:
Treats at Certain Hours:
opening the morning windows to sunlight and lemon groves,
a swim before lunch after a sunbath,
a nap after lunch and a walk after that,
and a wash and the bliss of shaving without necessity,
and the sweet smell of clean clothes . . .

then the descent to the concert,
to the little formal parlor,
a perfect set-up for receiving in-laws
or the mortician,
to the slow disappearance of brilliance (*adagio*)
and the slow entrance of coolness (*molto tranquillo*),
sitting before the yellow grin of the dial,
the wooden idol which told me, very young,
something of this world and the art of this world . . .

so that I lost myself in the sound and separation
as the cooking stoves grew hot
and along the shore, the cooling sand
darkened and accepted the waves' steady slap.

# LOOKING AT THE NIGHT

Lax and decrepit, the fountain figure—
washed by the moon—remembers itself as it was.

The path and table are renewed and plated.
The birdbath has become mercury.

There is a hush here by my window.
The small wind smells of nuts and grapes.

Chalk traveler, regarding the fields of evening,
whisper to me your pure improvisations.

# MORNING IN TARRAGONA

I CARRY my
plaited basket full
of empty bottles
down the hill
to get oil, wine
and petrol,
hugging the short shadows
next to walls,
walking through
a reassuring volley
of "good days."

All night
dark winds have
pulled at
our garden.

Now,
with the rising light,
the angels of strangeness
settle,
placating their enormous wings.

# VISITING

*Tibberton Court, near Gloucester*

SECOND visit. From this height
the wet familiar fields are slung westward
to May Hill with its memorial crown of trees
in full August leaf. I watch
the loaded clouds slowly reveal their scroll
of shadows across the farm's spread.
A rainy summer.

The tennis lawn is here—
its net drawn up and draped to show an ankle of space.
No games now. The players are gone.
The croquet hoops are here,
but the clonk of mallets belongs
to the tenants in the North Wing.

It's not the same is it? Time's a flirt.

Days of rain and warmth
have made the thick grasses quicken.
Second crops are ripe. Under
the ash tree that stands
at the spot where the field drops
mushrooms have sprung up.
Their milk chocolate ribs make us think
of whale's teeth, sea shells
and great architecture.

Friend, you live here. Have stayed
to return a thousand balls and pluck wild mushrooms.
To watch the nudging cows lick coarse grass

and savour the clover's cap. To cheer
the roses peering over the stable wall.

We stroll the grounds uneasily (I
a bit too fast with my snake-shy steps),
smile a lot, but have little to say.
Coming here again . . . well . . .
To be able at night to see
the grain lake, white with the moon's foam,
lap the balustrade!
To flush the whirring birds . . .

When the old trees sigh, time sings.
The roof of the church is autumnal
with its slates golden, raspberry, wine red.
Inside, the small church is cool. Used still.
A functioning bishop lives nearby.

The same names of past gardeners, farmers, heirs,
who walked once where we walk
between the lichen-tarnished stones,
wait for us.
Like us, adding
unnecessary shade.

# LONDON ROSES
*Russell Square*

My shoulder aching
from my army pack,
surplus and old
like my memory, quick
to remember for me and
tell my mind a child's story
of infantry maneuvers and roses.

Yes, roses! They were there
in the dry requisitioned acres
deep in Texas. Now deep
in my heart as I walk through
June London roses—going on thirty-nine.

Playful water plays
with jittery birds. Children dance
nearer and nearer—magnets
to its dazzle. Years
have gone by since
there was a war I was the age for.

I long, for no reason,
to lie in new grass, reading,
dozing under the same sky
over me now—beneath
similar great trees,
their skirts, their scarves, lovable
as the hems of girls.

Instead, I drop
into a chipped-paint chair.

There are no childhood orioles
or red-winged blackbirds dipping,
but I am thankful for this square.

Tea helps. I revive—
to see the roses in their historical present.
Near them, an Indian child is
so beautiful I have to smile
and share my smile with its mother.

I had wanted . . .
wanted to drift away, dreaming . . .
Never!

I get up,
walk over to touch
the vivid, immediate petals.

# LEAVING ENGLAND

*a.*
ENOUGH clouds for a storm.
A form sits on the wind,
silent, traveling, like a gull.

He stares.       Blank study.

To extract grace from that movement?
The love from her?

*b.*
The expanding sky
caused him to think
or imagine he thought.

He dreamed.
Poet
all at sea.

*c.*
Deep in spring country
green plumes heave.

He sees the probability of his death.
He knows the green ground has been green before.

### d.

Untouched but threatened,
two figures walk
through a golden tunnel at Hampton Court.

The words are white the moon speaks.
The long passage under the laburnam
sends down its yellow droplets.

She and he walk.
Intermittent light strikes them.

### e.

Poems are flying away like sailfish.
Beer bottles founder, sink.

The figure beside him should be
all the poem he needs.
Yet the hum persists,
the form hovers,
the wake churns,
the refuse dances.

# 2 P.M. GOING WESTWARD ON THE CHICAGO, BURLINGTON & QUINCY

THE farms are beautiful in this light,
the dry cropped stalks of corn an easy match,
in their expanse, for the big sky.
Red barns. Silver silos.
Land-colored horses blendings into the combed ground.
Great plumed clouds hauling a storm.
The trees' dark fingers spread for winter's clasp.

If the snow—which seems to be waiting
just outside—
chooses to come in lace blows,
I hope our tearing through them
in steady curving trails,
won't anger the god of patterns
or the god of white.

# THE FALLS: PETERBOROUGH

CALM before the drop,
of uncertain depth,
dark brown like syrup.

About ten feet from the lip
of the plunge a bright green
island of grasses means "shallow."

A weathered-gray wooden chair
waits, partly submerged, for
the final thrust over.

Catching the smooth wall of water
like clenched fists,
rocks sort the water into spray,

foam, streams, waves
that dance and drop, roaring
into an avalanche of glints.

All to slip into a pool
of thick bubbles, lacy scum
that keeps being re-woven

moving off at the edges
and speeding up
just before ending in pure air;

the fast water following
its banks toward the lower,
smaller falls and mill race

that shines
then dips
into a graceful curl—

all of it coming out even.

# FOR YOUR VASE

NOTE: *The phrase "itinerant Niagaras" in part a. of "For Your Vase" I owe to Marianne Moore. The "Carlo" named in part j. of the same sequence is a cat belonging to Mary Miller. Most of the "facts" in the poem "The King of the Wild Beasts" come from Janet Flanner's profile of Matisse originally published in* The New Yorker.

# FOR YOUR VASE

*a.*

THE great whale looms in the white waves,
carrying concerts of sea birds on his back,
*allowing* like the sweet lawns of the public parks.

Far off in the rangelands, thunderstorms move
like itinerant Niagaras.


*b.*

This time I thought:
"Will the moon hold out
against all that blue-black?"


*c.*

Safe from their sleep of winter,
lilies uncurl and call.
Shells dry on the shore.

In the haymow a finch fidgets.
Under an ash tree a tulip fires.

Soul, which wind transports you
to the distant mountains with their monkey music?


*d.*

Wind:
> Brook through this summer day.
> Convex of concave curtains.
> > Sap of sails.

*e.*

O clowns whose white faces blush with the roses of love!
O madonnas whose green faces are vessels for rose wine!
Is your mastery of the art of containment teachable?


*f.*

in May
ground, branch, stem, leaf, catch green and flare.
    Rooms exhale their winters,
    lawns raise constellations,
    trees start to whistle,
    lambs stand from dark knees.


*g.*

Boats are throbbing in the harbor
impatiently loading rich cargo.

You!

The real are things that can be loaded
or can be taken
or can be left.


*h.*

The moon hooked to its dark wall moves us:
limes singled out by sunshine from drenched leaves.

Or, in a darkened theatre,
one consuming the square of silence like fire.


*i.*

All summer the lake has been a sapphire,
hard blue and green that cannot be held or copied.

And the wind has written on it with its white ink.
And the sun has sown it with a thousand sparklers.

*j.*
Beauty is more than nude proportion:

Your mouth tasting of mint and the sea.
Your face lit by grass and geraniums.
Carlo surrounded by anemones.

Frost going "clang" in the leaves.


**k.**
O weeds! Mists! Carcasses!
The river carries you through my house.
The sky leans over you.

On my roof, the night crows float in the moonlight.
In my garden
the statues have forgotten their chores.

# OCTOBER

*to Katherine Anne Porter*

BLAZE and blue the color of ideal water.
Furniture of grove and yard altered—
hazed, burnished, rearranged to seat snow.

Lord, gleam awhile in the ember leaves;
enrich their sweet red carols;
sing in the bonfires;
smile in the seed of the grape.

# A PAINTING OR SONG OR BOTH

THE road is rose beside the river.
Wheat-colored horses are climbing the opposite hillside.
The current runs dark over silver.

A woman in yellow bends to the water,
her image lacy light below poplars.

Stars hide until dusk to surprise her.

# SENTRY SEURAT

"... there is no evidence that Seurat showed the faintest
interest in open-air painting till after he had spent his year
of military service at Brest; and it is characteristic of him that
the revelation of light should come to him as he gazed on the
sea during the hours of sentry duty." —*Sir Kenneth Clark*


HE stood and faced geometries of dancing,
of light in air and light upon the water.
Stiff, at attention, slow to decipher,
he learned from his solitude a disconnecting.

Patient, still, he broke down blizzards of color;
saw, through the cameras of his look-out eyes,
motes mix and promote images of order:
confetti figures thrown on a screen of skies.

Later, accused of poetry, he rejoined, "I apply my method."
(Dots so set down that distance blinds and binds them.)
He often returned to the seacoast to re-evoke them
and wash the studio light from eyes no longer on guard.

# LETTER TO PASTERNAK

"It was like listening to a horse describing how it broke
itself in."                                        —*Doctor Zhivago*

BELIEVE me, I understand your refusal
to be turned out of the paddock where you have always
         cantered—
boldly or gently, just enough to ease fear's bit,
just enough then, conjuring, to strike free and be utterly
         off.

Off to range the lowlands and the shorelines,
running unfenced in prodigies of freedom,
swift in the singing air, conjoined with music,
part of the general song which is the poets' cycle:

silence to speech: cry to articulation;
moving and taking fresh fences as they extend
their brutal come-ons, tireless in their successions—
over and over, until you are broken and concede.

And desire only to be admitted back into the dark pasture,
having known for a long time a deeper liberty:
migrating from vista to vista, galloping over the heartlands,
internally, secretly, as unrestricted as a stallion's shadow.

# THE NOVELIST AT HOME
# IN NEW JERSEY

*to Glenway Westcott*

HE is the wall of this place whose hair
has the look of splash from a puddle.

Here, where a catbird gives problems to prose,
stone wall becomes room, becomes home, becomes all
of him.

"When I die, I want to lie in that wall."
(The one by the road where grapes crawl and walnuts
huddle.)

He is the wall of this place, whose chest
is crooked and whose stance converses.

How many kinds of weather make a novel?
How many singers can sing exactly when wanted?

How many reds can penetrate the blue?
How explain the swing of sex, the bugle, the flair

of horses running through Hunterdon County,
the mythical waters of Broadway on which ships pass?

He is the wall of this place, whose eyes
are sky-held-in-check. Whose words are disordered order.

How many words to a house? How many houses turn hovels?
He is the wall of this place, whose haircut splashes,

who captures the tilt of heaven for his chapters,
whose novels lean and, in slow water, double.

# THE ICE CREAM HOUR
## Giuseppe di Lampedusa

> *"Les privileges de la naissance sont des privileges contre la naissance."*
> —Manzoni

OUTSIDE Mazzara's,
even now, carriages pause
at the Ice Cream Hour.
And waiters hustle out
hoisting trays of ices
to be eaten on the spot.

His shadow joins them,
but at a corner table,
in an inner room—
screened-off when there is
a family party going on.

To his table, from
morning into the dead hour
of Palermo afternoons,
would come what the Princess
called his "pupils."

He was forever reading or talking—
of "eternal Sicily, *nature's* Sicily,"
of his readings (with his wife,
in five languages),
of his ancient class with its "low
consumption of general ideas."

Often he talked with his cousin
the poet Luccio Piccolo
who wrote *Canti Barocchi,* living
at (what a name!) Capo d'Orlando.

Sometimes, weighed down
by Sicilian sadness, the loss
of family palaces,
he sat and pined.
The Princess suggested that he write
of what he loved that was gone.

He began.

So, *Il Gattopardo.* So
the "memories of light,"
of things more than people.
Places of his infancy,
meandering through a lost Earthly Paradise . . .

All written to the reader who,
he wrote, "won't exist."
Such positive use of the future!
That future—he couldn't imagine—
which was there, waiting to arrive,
filled with us.

# THE KING OF THE WILD BEASTS
## *Henri Matisse*

RARE painter who prefers the sunlight,
he stirs in his bed and orders the shutters opened
after another night asleep and awake
watched by the radio, the night nurse and a hundred
                    drawings,
and wishes for more time.

Sleepless, impatient with the waste of darkness,
he has studied the drawings with a flashlight
and found that there is so much distance to cover
if he is ever to reach Marseilles before nightfall.

The first fig marigold in the hotel park
quivers in the sunshine like a lover.

It has never amused him to amuse himself.
The birds whistle.
A woman arranges her stocking.
It is very late.
The winter on the mountains melts into summer.
Though he no longer has to hesitate,
he must combat facility that comes with age.

The chapel is finished. The hired Rolls gone from the drive.
A lady in Paris remarks he is not a genius
because he has no interest other than painting.
His art is happy, but who knows his mind?
He whispers to Mme. Lydia, *"J'ai le trac!"*

The light of New York was like crystal.
The light of Tahiti altogether different.

Where your work is, there is your paradise.
Where your light is, there is your work.
The sun-inspected world will prove in shadow
what can withstand its light.

Now he inspects the day. The far boats wait.
The birds contain their songs in the shivering trees.
Among the stations of the imagination
Marseilles is only one of many places.
He wonders if he will reach or recognize it
or if that one place is
the one he has always wanted most to visit.
And there is so much distance to cover before nightfall
if he is ever to reach that fugitive harbor,
designing the very landscape through which he travels.

# EARLY LIGHT

*in memory of Edward Hopper*

WHEN we get up in the morning
we feel for an unmeasured second
that the new light and our new look around
mean that we are only just then beginning,

that what happened last night or yesterday,
even last month, even last year,
didn't happen; that we are new born,
newly boarding this earth with our loaded bags.

The past is no longer a succession of regrets
about the time in which we did nothing, about
which we can do nothing.
No!

In the morning's early light we see things
never seen before (by us in any event)
and we are full of joy and possibilities.

# IN THE
# FINANCIAL DISTRICT

# IN THE FINANCIAL DISTRICT

THE Customs House is like a giant music box
a-tinkle with starlings.
Pigeons are roosting on a lot of nearby ledges.
As far as I can see, white collars perch
at every human throat around here.

They are tearing buildings down
in order to put buildings up—
here in the Financial District.

I live in the Financial District.

They are digging a hole one block south
of where I live
and when they have finished that,
they will pile up stories
and my narrow view of the Ferry Landing
and the river will be walled-off.

I seem to spend my life living on low floors.
What makes me live in New York then I wonder?
I even worked once on the third floor
of the Empire State Building.
That was embarrassing I can tell you!

Yes, it turns out that I'm a low-story dweller
in a high-story city.
At least so far.

I don't imagine there's very much I can do about it.
Except get rich and move up higher.

But poets don't get rich and I think
I'd miss looking up at all the big buildings.
Especially down here in the Financial District
where the buildings have turned into silos
in my imagination. Silos where they store green money—
billions and billons of dollars worth—
against some rainy day.

I once tried to guess how much money *is* stored
away in these tall buildings, but
I'm no good at guessing games.
Other people always win the jawbreaker-count.
I just turn all that money invisible in my mind.
And then I get the sense of it.
I often walk through drifts of it like snow dunes,
or kick it along like fallen leaves.

On weekends the refuse truck passes
as noisy as the racket of heroes, echo-amplified,
its green maw chewing its way between the offices,
and it chomps up a good deal of the money.
But there's always more where that came from!
Usually, there's no one around to see the
refuse truck eat its way along—or even hear it—
except me maybe:
It sometimes startles a scabby drunk
besides me, asleep in my ivory loft.

# IN THE REDWOOD FOREST
*Muir Woods*

THROUGH these green Parthenons
small birds assert their levels,
measuring their heights and heavens
in tireless flights.
Light hangs like grapes sweating in thick gloom.
Failures of sunshine abdicate the air,
give up their falling halfway down.

As I go deeper, like them, into obscurity,
all around me the light plunges and wrecks,
until even sound seems affected by darkening
and I begin to hear my being alone.

I stop to look all the way up
and suddenly feel at the bottom of someplace—
as if I'd changed places with the stones
I looked down at earlier,
watched stare up at me through
the brown, clear stream
that cuts its lifetime into
the dimming strata.

# A MAN CHANGING HIS LIFE

It's not so bad, really,
being broke.
You have less to decide about.
You're doing your own work.

Shops have taken on a new lustre:
they've become galleries.
You look, enjoy, or doubt.
What to eat is not much of a problem.
For laughs there's always the Theater of Streets.

Nights, sometimes, when you haven't made out,
the going gets rough.
But there's lots less of a hangover.
Beers add up too fast.
Your pocket tells you when you've had enough.

Does anything stay the same
with you so "different"?
There seems to be less worry
about what other people have.
And yet, toward the gods you are still defiant.

# WINTER FIGURES

I WAS up near Fifth at the zoo.
Cold but nice on the terrace.
I'd eaten out.

Returning to work I stopped
to watch the sun shake in spokes—
a pattern of drops wheeling
off the wet seals who seemed
to be sewing their pond.

Then coming away, I saw,
near the place where ponies draw carts,
an old man drop a bag
and shiver carefully down
toward the ground.

From the care he took
in grasping what was left of the grain
unscattered,
his rage at the way the pigeons
burst up all around him like new crops,
it was clear he'd come to feed them.

But in his own way,
at his own speed,
and the design in his mind
important.

# SONG OF MORNING COFFEE

Hello. It is a good day.
A bowser walks a boy on a chain.
No chance of rain. Clear skies.

I am praying the morning paper
which has sounds of praise in it.
It welcomes the fact of the visitor-sun
always coming to call.

"Clear skies" it says here in the *Times*.
I see it's true. I agree.
Skies fit for Aristophanes' silly birds to meet in.
Skies for the likes of me.
I thank you.

I think when I finally wake up
I'll be a person more than I am,
be ideal, be better able to grasp the situation
(which is a sunny morning),

to say, not just words, but to speak,
to sit as a sitter, to drink as a drinker,
to be here, to be really awake,
to be able to sing my little song:

> My beard is on my razor
> My coffee's in its cup
> The ghosts well-hid in the draperies
> I'm up.

Best to keep at it. It would
be stupid to let it go.

The hot liquid travels.

The sun fondles.

Forget the honest voices of night!

# HIGH WIND AT THE BATTERY

THE corner bank has lost a great window.
Pete's lunch counter has shattered glass
sitting in its booths.
All the flags are straining horizontally
and the huge crane at Water Street is nodding

because down here at the toe-end of Manhattan
the February winds are howling,
having left the Plains States a few days ago
but not the least bit tired from the trip.

Feeling none too safe in my loft
tucked between tall buildings,
I look up quickly at each shudder of a window,
at every lash of the loose aerial against the glass.

The pigeons, whose roaring coos wake
me up all the time, are keeping quiet
and nervous in several corners. There are
a couple of them outside my bathroom not even
being sexy—apprehensive as hell.

We're always being surprised by weather in this city,
always unprepared for anything natural,
like a rainstorm or a blizzard or, now, this wild wind—
living so much behind walls and traveling around in tunnels.

But I have to admit the wind does excite me.
I'm sorry I'm not at the top of one of these buildings
so I could see things blowing around,

the water arching its back at being rubbed the wrong way,
smoke from ships' stacks looping in every direction.

As a matter of fact, wind like this means
that for a short time the air will be fresher,
that the city is getting a needed dusting—
means that we're that much nearer to slow-coming spring.

# ONE OF THE WONDERS

At those special hours in summer,
after afternoon and just before evening,
when a salmon light leaps the west side of buildings,
what's left of my view of the river
clears
in a particular way
and becomes
as intensified as the sunset roofs of Venice.

This is one of the wonders of New York—
to anyone who's lived here long enough
to notice,
to hate and then despair of
and then love
this hard city, splendid
by its lordly waters.

Office people hurry pleasantly through
the narrow streets
bent
for the ferry to Staten Island—
a lift to their step and
the corners of their mouths
even though they are dead-on-their-feet
and dog-tired.

(Quite a contrast to their quicker
but slower step in the morning
when—even though they look rested
and fresh-pressed—they are easily spotted
as heading The Wrong Way.)

Do they find time or clear-enough thoughts
to note
the million-dollar color they're hurrying through?
Which does not happen every evening
and never twice the same?

Or is this transforming glory
which makes their city Something Else
and connects them with treasure,
unseen
by them as they run
to catch the champing ferry

which will take them away,
with their backs to
this rose miracle,
to hot dinners, soothing whiskey, and
loving arms?

# LOOKING AT THE
# EMPIRE STATE BUILDING

It is still The Tallest Building in the World.
(Although they are already busy changing that.)
Coming as I do from the Great Plains,
it has been my Holy Mountain from the beginning.
When it disappears past clouds, I imagine
the gods holding a picnic—for once
happily masked from our stares.

At night when the top is lighted
I see it as my Holy Volcano
and the biggest penny-bank anywhere.
It is the only present I would ever
have liked to give Jean Harlow.
Planes and birds are known to crash into it.

I can't help expecting any minute
to see poor King Kong fall from the dirigible mast
or spot lovely Melisande leaning out from an upper floor
to let down her long golden hair.

# ON SEEING THE MOVIE VERSION OF
# H. G. WELLS' *THINGS TO COME* (1936)
# AGAIN (MARCH 1967)

IT becomes clearer, as time goes along,
that it has changed for us:
what a "long time" is,
what is possible "in time," are different
expressions than they once were.

Startling to sit in the dark and watch
a movie made in 1936 about an endless war
that shrinks to endless little wars (we
call them "contained") and
to see a series of giant dates hinge
up one by one onto the screen, striking
obviously thirties poses—1955 . . . 1960 . . .
1967 . . . (which is now!)

Where they stop after 27 years
of fighting—when the New Men
put an end to the last warrior hold-outs
and begin a new Age of Reason and Peace.

Then a jump to the next century—
2070—and attractive, sexy, slightly
Roman clothing (thirties make-up
on the men though) with imaginative
futuristic cities and factories:
the Triumph of Science and The Mind.

And it's time to shoot for the moon at last.
But a pretty bad sculptor who represents
the Dissenting Artist and wears nostalgic clothes
a little like costumes for a 19th Century Prospero,

decides there is more to life than Progress
and it's time to cry "halt!" to this
heartless sacrifice of young people
just to satisfy our curiosity about the moon—
Who wants to go to the moon anyway?

(Well, the young people want to go—
more than anything. As a matter of fact,
two of the Top People's children!—a girl
and young man who love each other.)

So he rouses a mob and they try to wreck
the Space Gun. But the heroes are too fast for them
and with a great roar the lovers
are shot into space.

And that's where the picture ends
except for a little pleasant philosophy
spoken by Raymond Massey in classic profile
against a field of night sky with stars.

That was 1936 and Wells wrote his own screen play.
And this is only 1967 and we are still fighting.
But we're not going to wait for another hundred years
to go to the moon. No sir! We're going to shoot for it
any day now.

Oh dear H.G.W., how I wish we had all the time
you thought we had!

# ODE TO POLLYANA

THOU sunny, undefatigable pal of cheerfulness,
child of happiness, fool of joy,
I have these new glasses
that I want to tell you about:

rather than rose they are sun-colored
and I am looking through them right now at a sunny world.
"Astro-matic—the only automatic ski glass" the name and
               claim.
The glass changes color according to brightness.
Can you imagine what the snowy mountains must look like
all golden whizzing past?

Stand there sweetly disguised as Mary Pickford
and listen to my song of happiness.
I can't help it.
Today I am looking
and I love everything I see.
All knowledge, all criticism, I'm overlooking.

Oh it's a great day!
Through my yellow glasses the trees are vivid
and the grass looks painted.
The sky is green and the red lights are all orange.
I'm looking forward to seeing everything for the first time.

Up to now things have not been looking any too good lately.
But now, thanks to a miracle of science,
my natural optimism and cheeriness
(which I don't have to tell *you* about)

can come into their deserving own.

I just discovered even lights at night become sunshine!
I have to take it easy and look at things one by one.
Come on along little girl!
We'll walk all around this city
and take turns wearing my sun glasses.

*TOWARD*

# AT A FUNERAL NOT MY MOTHER'S

How long ago was it she lay down?
It was nineteen hundred and forty one.
A war was moving across the world.
I've never remembered the kind of weather.

Now another ceremony troubles me
and I drop to my knees without thinking,
without thinking of any prayers or words,
just conscious of some dirt and twigs

breaking under the pressure of my knees;
of a clump of grasses spreading to live, to wait
like some conquered village to rise again;
of the brown earth reminding me of my mother's hair.

Hair stamped down, bent, dead, like a wig
instead of the warm cloud I once passed
across my face, once pulled by hand.

Since then winds have thawed my sails
and sent me here and there in a rush
always toward . . . toward . . .

Toward this, today,
my kneeling here—
at last fully conscious of
terrible
        cold.

# INHABITING

Every day is the practice
of pretending to be in it—

where it is
in the concrete sense:
city, street, building, room, body,
year, month, week, day, hour, minute.

You, he, she, or the radio
may be "present,"
but I am not here
though my body is.

I am learning the charming smile
of all travelers.

Who will wear my body
while it stays?

# NEAR DROWNING

Loss of weight.
Sensation of other air.
Tightening,
           sinking,
stiff with fright;
                dropping
until the bottom frees you at last
and you retake the surface and its dare.

Then down again,
               down,
                    down,
as if falling was the only direction
your
      body                           with all your might
         knew,
                    up again
        to
          push

                      scaling heights that
vanish as you climb . . .

The waves' white hands
clap for you to stay!

A great lion is gathering to leap.

*You* leap,
dash,

roll,
shudder onto sand,
and somehow claim it—

        holding,
        holding
        to keep.

# NAKED

TAKE everything off
and stand in the sun.
Watch sweat begin to run
like streams washing down
into your valleys.

Change what you've been going as.
Drop the outfit you're wearing.
The more the clear light covers you
the more you'll be able to act.

Day by day
you have been going about
things.
Let them alone.

What comes between me and you,
what we actually think,
what we actually do,
will dress us.

# WORDS

PROMISES, lies,
sift, with the face that speaks them,
down to the dust created to become them.
Words stay.

The winter gull flies inland,
fleeing from grappling ocean.
He will repeat his flight until caught.

Endings! Endings!

Words are stronger.
Loss, distortion, blast
live long.
Words longer.

# TO WORDS

THEY have said, "too risky"
They have said, "too easy"
They have said, "your enemy is impatience"
They have said, "you're changing."

The shadows continue to bolster objects.
Every noon the hands of the clock meet again.

Come words!
and nourish the surprises of order.

Take on your lives
and live them with me.

Together, who knows?
we may last awhile.